HALF A MIND

Also by Mark Robinson

The Horse Burning Park
(Stride 1994)

A Hole Like That: 13 Cleveland Poets
(Editor, Scratch 1994)

Running Good Writing Groups
(with Rebecca O'Rourke, University of Leeds 1996)

Gaps Between Hills
(with Dermot Blackburn and Andy Croft, Scratch 1996)

HALF A MIND

Mark Robinson

FLAMBARD

Acknowledgements

Some of these poems have appeared in the following publications:
Blade, Fat Chance, First Draft and *Final Draft, Gairfish,*
Gaps Between Hills, Other Poetry, Poetry Ireland Review, The Rialto,
Smiths Knoll, Tenth Muse, The Wide Skirt and *Write On (Evening Gazette).*

'On the beach near Kinvarra our babies' is for Emily Stevens and her
family; 'Drinking alone in a pub in Bamber Bridge' for June Robinson,
with apologies and love; 'I think of you with nothing on' gratefully
recognises a debt to Adrian Mitchell and the Bluetones;
'The sea's rising arc' is for John Bosley and the Albert Poets, with thanks
for the typo; 'The family as the first soviet, and other daft ideas'
for Andy Croft; 'Sooner or later we must face the pittering crackle'
for Terry Lawson; 'Laying a Carpet With My Dad' for Alan Robinson.

Special thanks are due to Bernard and Mary Loughlin, and everyone at
The Tyrone Guthrie Centre, where many of these poems were written.
'Annaghmakerrig Kelpie' is dedicated to Bernard. Thanks also to
Northern Arts for the Writer's Award that made that trip possible,
and to Jenny Attala and Chrissie Glazebrook for all their help.

Flambard Press wishes to thank Northern Arts for its financial support.

First published in Great Britain in 1998 by Flambard Press
4 Mitchell Avenue, Jesmond, Newcastle upon Tyne NE2 3LA

Typeset by Barbara Sumner
Cover design by Claire Sanderson
Author photograph by Dermot Blackburn
Printed in Great Britain by The Cromwell Press,
Broughton Gifford, Melksham, Wiltshire

A CIP catalogue record for this book is available from the British Library.
ISBN 1 873226 27 6
© 1998 Mark Robinson

Contents

I: Bringing Down the Government

II: Voice-overs

III

I

Bringing Down the Government

*for Alison, of course,
and Louis and Billie*

Today is Sunday, and for that reason
the idea comes into my head, the sobbing into my breast
and into my throat a kind of great lump.
Today is Sunday, and this
is centuries old, otherwise,
it would be Monday, and the idea would come into my heart,
the sobbing into my brain
and into my throat a frightful longing to stifle
what I feel now,
man that I am and having suffered as one.

César Vallejo

I'm trying to be happy
and find it can be done.

Michal Cernik

There are messages to send:
gatherings and songs.
Because we need
to insist. Else what are we
for? What use are we?

Tess Gallagher

A political art, let it be
tenderness

Leroi Jones

Bringing Down the Government (Prologue – 1984)

'I've been loving you since the miners' strike...' (Soho)

By the time this house has a sea view, and we only
visit the park to recall the kids' paper boats
floating off like illustrations of the wind,
the moment for declarations of love will have passed,
be merely a reference to right now, a shorthand way
to explain lives grown somehow unusual.

We will do nothing all day but sit and wait
for richer friends to return from trips abroad.
Struggle and passion will be nostalgia. The meetings
we snuck out of will be forgotten. It will be like
breathing in and never feeling the breeze behind your rib cage.
It will be as dull as a Sunday spent on a bus.

If we could stop now to pinch the atmosphere
with these urgent fingers, we'd know something
was out of control. It feels like a harmonica solo
swerving past logical limits. It feels like steam in a kettle.
The seas are rising, we don't much care, and nothing
is going to be the same again. Know what? – I love you.

The seas are rising. The summer has blistered my nose
in a new way this year, and that's only the beginning.
The times are decadent and oblivious – it's either funny
or something beyond that, that hurts. What we're most
concerned with is spending more time together,
bringing down the government, and learning to stop smirking.

Know what? – I love you. Come
lean on me and watch us stop the future and its tide.
In the distance, if we can take our eyes off each other
for a second, you will see some glowing horizon.
That's where we're headed. That's the big plan.
What we do, what we do with it, is down to us.

I want to work something out:

the realist chaos of the market place,
its tired mugs and hawkers,
the lines, curves, noises and lights
struggling to mean something, a phrase
wheezed out, out of energy, a sham
of a shadow of a mockery of a sham,

has that anything to do with the engine
running beneath my window
and the marks left on the road tomorrow,
the barking that could be a child
hyperventilating through the unspeakable,
if it was not outside where the dog always barks?

I want to work something out.
I don't like to let the sun go down
on a dead end that means mayhem in my dreams.
No one hears my outsized collection
of sardonic jokes when I air them.
I'm glad. I can feel my mouth opening

and closing and the world just carry on.
I want to work something out.
Why I am stood over here when I want
to be over there in a heap with them.
Why I have started overusing the sound I.
Why I don't just shut the fuck up.

This is a travesty of a mockery of a sham.
This is the bottom of the hill
where the cheap light from the high street
ends its search, desperately squawking
as it corkscrews its frantic circles:
'What's the Big Idea? What's the Big Idea?'

As I pack the last of the LPs

the fractious excitement of the unknown
unfolds before us like the A19 in the dark:
you only know it's there when the light shines on it.
This is the grown-up move, where we learn
how much junk we've got we daren't throw away.

We sit among the boxes and the pictures stacked
like so many slices of bread, drink
the last gin, remember when we'd just arrived,
wondering what we will leave behind
for the next couple to exorcise.

In the kitchen there's the smell of garlic
and the dents in the wall where once,
tightening the cupboard doors back on,
I drew blood with the screwdriver,
nearly broke my hand hammering the wall.

The bedroom's bare boards echo, and oddly
it's the time spent ill in bed with chickenpox
that seems to have lingered beneath the rugs,
not the nights we conceived the children,
or the patient painful first times after.

If we've done things wrong here, we forgive ourselves.
When you shut the door and pop the keys through,
all the hours and events we thought were as solid
as my forehead are proved to be dreams
of other lives we might once have led:

we take a last peep through the blinds
we know they hate and expect to see
ourselves moving about, making tea,
putting on a record, dancing, making love,
like clips in an ad for a new film, about us.

Your nightmare unspeakable and mine dull,

still ready to punch the shining daylights
from the dreams that shocked us awake,
we stand on the doorstep and waste our breath
into metaphorical shapes in the cold air
that has gathered to greet us today.

Someone nearby is singing, raising their voice
to praise love's simple effects and movement.
It's a fine voice, pure and high, that comes
from a secret part of the brightening day.
I can see the song drifting over the gardens

bobbing and weaving around the trees
and the garages, caressing the burglar alarms
into silence and gentleness, fading
as it stretches out towards the playing fields.
I close the door and it stops. Then echoes

in our house that has yet to fully awaken.
Uninvited, wrapped in the leaves of the weather,
it circles above us again and again
while we breakfast alone then slowly
wake the children and lead them bleary-eyed

outside to listen to the song still
tilting its hips around the neighbourhood.
I wait for some kind of pay-off,
some dissonant note, but it doesn't come.
Today we will hold our tongues and enjoy.

Today the sky is flat

but you are not, you are almost perfect,
part the air as you walk to leave a calm
following like the wake and gulls behind a ferry.

But from behind your back you produce the pan
I burnt the aduki beans in, tender
bean-shaped holes stippling its black bottom.

I'm always getting things wrong: the world
is full of things struggling to be metaphors
for the exact opposite of everything I dream of.

Sometimes I think I only do this to encourage
the world to be other than it is.
I keep on looking at things as if I imagined them.

I'm trying to stop. I'm sorry about the pan.
In the poem I was writing it was full of water.
It was only just starting to boil.

Song I

A whiskey & water
a gin on the rocks
a vodka & orange
a rum & black
a fistful of aspirin
for the morning –
and one for yourself.

A bacardi & coke
a brandy & soda
three fingers of bourbon
a tequila slammer
a foolproof disclaimer
for the morning –
and one for yourself.

A hemlock shandy
a strychnine spritzer
a turps & Tizer
a paraquat & Perrier
and a poultice
for my saintly fevered brow –
and one for yourself.

On the beach near Kinvarra our babies

play on the slate-grey sand.
The football rebounds from the surf
again and again. And again
the spite-sapping wind carries it back,
gently back to our son's excited arms.

I try to clamber out into the foam
along the ragged teeth of the rocks,
but the sand sucks at my unsuitable shoes,
like in Lou's favourite bedtime story
of my escape from building-site mud.

You can't stop laughing, keep repeating
'Typical, just exactly typical.'
The sun goes down and turns
the woman gathering Lucky Stones
into a shadow who waves goodbye.

The children chase each other up the slope
to where the seaweed meets the tarmac.
As we negotiate the tortuous roads
to this fortnight's home, they sleep.
We talk of your plans for the garden.

Something pretty. Something indestructible.
The sea returns the ball we left behind.
It rolls down through the weed, floats back.
Rolls down again, is pushed stubbornly back,
until it stays where it has been put.

Shivering under blankets in the car

we wonder if we really want to go back.
A four-hour wait and the sea's cutting up,
folding stiff peaks clumsily under black water,
knocking the holiday from us before we're even home.
It's finally happened: all the lights in England are out.

Containers shunt their mysteries from place
to place while every few minutes the man in front
jerks out to stamp his feet and slap his palms.
You try to read by the driver's light, and
I find I can recall all but one of my old class.

Aspinall, Aspinall, Bailey, Bainbridge, Chessal...
There was someone between Myers and me –
of all the names I should remember that one.
After an hour of calling the register I crack it:
Reid. But what was his first name? So many

wet lunchtimes shared on the dull backfields
and I can't even remember their real names.
Reid. Reidy. Into heavy metal later. Odd:
not a single one I could call up, I realise,
if we were going back there. I know – David.

As dawn approaches and we start to stretch
our aches into the shape of a question ending
How much longer? it's as if some surly jobsworth
nearing the end of a double shift has passed
his dirty brush across the still foreign sky.

And all the real clouds are being delayed
on the other side of the Channel,
over some miserable teenager's house.
We have no choice but to go back
and find them, and blow them all away.

An April morning gathers itself

the way you straighten your shirt and walk down
to the kitchen. Your bowl chimes against the nail
holding the leaf of the table together.
The mist that was hiding the school playground
clears and the brightness of the day starts to hum
like the rim of a glass under a graceful finger.

The children and I walk the idea of fun
from one end of the park to the other
but it never quite learns to run on its own.
Back home we kick a ball around the garden
to stay out of your way but my mind's set
on other things and I can see you fidgeting.

It feels like weeks since yesterday,
the resolutions, intentions and gin,
the sofa supporting us in whatever we did,
the stairgate coming off right that very minute –
feels like the door we timidly opened is swinging
slowly but surely back in our surprised faces.

By dinnertime the sun is swollen and fierce,
high enough to look down on our compromise.
We think too much about things, we agree,
or not enough, or just the right amount but badly.
The floor we polished before the kids woke up
gets covered with beans that glow in the sunlight.

I can tell I've got that look on my face

that makes your face go quiet and still –
can be in the kitchen chair looking out
at what is, despite all, a fine morning,
when I feel it tick at the left side of my face,
like some invisible thread had been sewn
through my cheek, just where my beard stops

when I haven't shaved, and something is tugging it.
It's not painful or even uncomfortable,
I just become aware of it and know
that somehow it's an unpleasantness
I could do without. It's not simple and
it can't be worked through. It surfaces

the way the slang of a colony slides
blissfully into official language.
I'm not sure, though, if I don't prefer this
to the elaborate smirk that breaks through
when I try to tell you a lie or talk
of a woman I really rather fancied.

I'm not sure, either, if I want to think that
people can feel the looks they carry settle.
Even these days I still run to the mirror
to check, though I couldn't say quite what,
or why the face always there still surprises,
that of an old friend I thought I'd forgotten.

Song II: Under the Settee

Two empty crisp packets
(Worcester Sauce)
A Batman bearing *Good News*
From Readers Digest!
Dog hairs even though
we don't have a dog

A toy fire engine
painted muddy brown
Some long-lost toe nails,
the scissors
Fag ends even though
neither of us smoke

The pink and bitten lid
from the rabbit cup
A knife, a spoon,
a plate and a fork
A sausage roll even though
we don't eat meat

A small attempt
at civilisation
developed under
a very low ceiling
Utopias even though
we have taken to pragmatism

Drinking alone in a pub in Bamber Bridge

something, perhaps the jukebox, reminds you
there is a promised land, and it looks like this,
but this is not it. This is a thin Tuesday night
in the town of your birth, in October,
a breech and bruising birth, for which
your mother has never quite forgiven you.

You are looking for old friends in a strange pub.
If you asked, the barman would point people out.
The one with his foot in his mouth, laughing.
The one with the face like a wet Wakes Week.
You sit in the corner alone. The songs pass
like years. You search for something good

to put on, but there's not even Elvis.
In this pub at least Elvis is still and always
dead, a small excuse for their dad's sideburns.
The Massed Beer Mat Flippers of Bamber Bridge
are all the welcome home you can find,
and nobody, but nobody recognises you.

You start to draw the road out of here,
but it will dry on the table and leave a slug trail
that will give you away. Your parents will find you.
The Flippers grin as if in on one of your secrets,
that even you have forgotten: the silhouettes
inside a tent at a party, the wild gossip in the house.

As you leave you see the buses cross the bridge
into town, splashing the puddles into the river.
The water drops through the bridge's dark shadow
like rain onto the taut canvas of that tent,
the slap like the feet of a man running, running,
a series of nails driven rapidly home.

As we continue our search for pomegranates

the rain drenches the crowded market stalls
with all the descriptive detail it can muster.
Sometimes home can be the most exotic place
there is, the shoppers' faces as wrinkled
and misshapen, as fascinating as the oldest
babushkas in the remotest Uzbeki village.

Today is not one of those days. Today
is a shop-for-fruit and get-the-hell-out day.
Buskers stare forlornly from Barratt's
doorway, weighing up the pros and cons
of electrocution, their chances of survival.
The pineapples, girls, are guaranteed sweet.

The pomegranates in their boxes nestle
in shredded raffia, hold more promises
than anyone could ever keep. They'll spill
their bitty regrets into the folds of your shirt,
will stain it the colour of my bitten lips.
In the morning you'll wonder how that happened.

The Gazette shouts, or at least raises its voice,
to tell us of cheap gas, plummeting power prices.
There is no power here, no power at all.
Today is one of those days the town seems
inhabited purely by stroke victims, ourselves
included. We poke each other in the ribs:

it's like being seventeen again, drifting
round cafés bored and superior. We're not.
There's something difficult and puzzling
about the sequence of the traffic lights
at the crossroads: we find ourselves stranded,
hold out our hands as if to check it's still raining.

Between the cat food and the secateurs

my reflection winks back from a cracked wing mirror,
out in the garage, beating a hollow into a pile of papers.
The dark outside disapproves of the figure I cut
while you are coping, the rhythm that I've set up.

Fuck it. If I knew what to say next,
when I stick my head on a pole and offer it
through the back door as an apology, I wouldn't be here.
I wouldn't have bothered to have muddied my shoes.

Wind blows through the rowing machine that couldn't
get rid of my beer gut. The hammering from a neighbour's shed
echoes my thrashing the headlines, drops into the hole
I'm ripping in this four-foot pile of bad news, ridiculous.

The Neighbourhood Watch peeps through the cat flap, concerned.
Go home, please. There's nothing to see now.
A drunken man contemplating the differences
between a monkey wrench and a tin opener.

Something vague has somethinged me

I'm not sure when and I don't care to check.
Sometime between that first kiss in the damp
and swirling basement of Everton Boys Club
and now, this soggy mass of in-between
that feels all the time like afterwards.

Let this spoil our late-night reading of the papers:
you are what you do, not what you dream of doing.
Our dreams most would not recognise if
they waved a flag, which they do: a big red one
with a picture of James Brown and Elvis on it.

Glasses half-empty, or full, whatever, we're drunk
and bent on uncovering the truth to all this.
This is my dream: us together naked
in a railway-station photo booth after midnight,
and while we wait for the photos to slide out,

phallic and glistening, ready to steal our fingerprints,
delayed passengers queue to pat us on the back
and scribble on our goose-bumped flesh
with indelible marker pens. 'Dreamers' it says
on my thighs and across your shoulders.

Meanwhile, outside in our dreams, and outside
in our drunkenness, the day whips its energies
into a whirlwind with us at its centre.
We're not the centre of anything, we blush,
but it takes not a blind bit of notice.

Song III

Give him a hammer to seal his window.
Give him a bag to hide his head.
Give him a sock to seal his mouth.
Give him an axe for under the bed.
If the bastard's not guilty, why is he bleeding?

Take his TV and beat it to bits.
Take his diaries and show them around.
Take his good name and use it in vain.
Take his secrets and make sure they're found.
If the bastard's not guilty, why is he bleeding?

Make his money earn its keep.
Make his smile seem winning.
Make his story almost dull.
Make his lies like sinning.
If the bastard's not guilty, why is he bleeding?

And if he squeals don't let him go.
And if he asks don't let him know
And if he weeps don't let tears flow.
And if he denies show him it's so.
If the bastard's not guilty, why is he bleeding?

After eighteen years of this sort of thing

I will put my best heart forward and hope
for a dip in the attentions of the day.
The rational city plays a peeping game
behind the headlines and the U-turns,
our friends' necessary betrayals.

The reversals, the blockage, the lost
and irreplaceable gather at our gate,
like snails that crunch under the children's feet.
The afternoon feels like an in-joke
no one can fully explain. I'm so tired

of being English in this shabby excuse
for what might be, so thoroughly tired
of feeling like a man questioning the rules
of cricket or football – why *can't* he touch it
with his hand? – I can hardly breath these words.

But if I've inherited one thing from
my family it's a stubborn streak as wide
as the Ribble. I am going to sit here until
the image of Portillo at the stake
disappears from my morbid mind.

And then tomorrow you and I will take the kids
to the allotment, where we will plant sunflowers
on our communal land to mark the beginning
of the end. To such small victories am I reduced.
The light fades suddenly, is swallowed by evening.

I think of you with nothing on,

the shyness and boldness of curves
that have tipped me up and swung me round
until my head was full of ringing feedback
and those arched and tempting eyebrows
luring us over a faintly marked border
into the autumn-soaked field of the new.

I think of you and miss you now, the pot
of your belly that fits into my hot palm,
the unregarded navel wrinkled and winking,
self-conscious from two dramatic labours,
like a pruning scar on the bole of a tree,
the symmetry of the stretch marks on hips

and belly, silver stabs of tension that pull
and grow even now when the children tug away,
that concertina to next to nothing, a rouche
of darker skin that curls back from my fingertips,
a tenderness we dare hardly speak,
until you lie down and all lines shift.

I have started to thicken, to set
into the shape of my dad, can feel
the temptation grow to whip out my denture
at a quiet unexpected moment, the way
my grandad used to, to embarrass my nan.
I'm holding my belly in as I write this

so you won't misunderstand: I think of you
and want you here to pose this question:
haven't these concessions been worth it?
It's hard to believe this nakedness,
or the thought of it, won't lead somewhere,
isn't an image for how we must carry on.

You think it's laughable the way

I count on touchable things to save us.
There are eight young lads playing football
on the grass between the council houses.
In the phone box that's one of their posts,
a teenage boy is arranging a date,
away from the leers of his family.

By the time the weekend collapses
out of breath, with its lungs burning,
he'll have moved up a league, will know
something serious has happened. He'll start
to imagine chaos into a comedy
to recall as a totem when he's older.

He'll make it up. He'll forget it wasn't true.
Not such a bastard, but he'll forget her real name.
We always want something more than we have.
The ties swollen like knots in rope have roots
in the garden, that tangle the trees and earth us.
I want fulfilment now, for everyone, or not at all.

The baby alarm broadcasts our broken night
to the plates and bottles in the living room,
the unused places we set at the table.
The packet of fig rolls by our bed as dry
and tempting as a hungover kiss
was sincerely meant to prove my intentions.

I've half a mind, and that's all I need,

to turn this street upside down
and hide in the warmth of ignorance,
not a thought for how the light squeezed
from good homes drains down, disappears
through the sloping grass to the river.

I could sit there and ghost a stranger's life,
slip in some things I've admitted to no one,
cross my fingers certain people never read it.
You. Moving through events not your own
you can slip off the shackles a while.

I can ramble on until I meet this stranger's
friends, his lovers. In a place that feels
like a corner I find his family huddled together
for warmth, though they are bickering fiercely.
They're making up insulting names for him, or me.

I'm so tired you could snuff me out
with a simple bringing together of your thumb
and forefinger. It wouldn't even hurt.
The street is no duller than any other
in England, but it rankles. The sun

ducking down beyond the park is like
a smear of egg yoke on a child's bib.
The dusk goes into meltdown, into
feedback, and then it starts to rain,
big, petulant globs of rain that in a minute

turn to hail and back again, to tattoo
a state-of-the-nation broadcast
down the back of my neck, that's steam
in a moment and heard no more.
I've half a mind, and that's all I need...

Song IV: Unite...

You have nothing to lose but
your trespasses and thoughts of trespasses
your envy of the road home
your turning mind and its churning mulch
your domestic epiphanies
your overdraft

Nothing to lose but
your struggle for ways to struggle
your unusable witticisms
your notebook for clinching detail
your bin and the crap stuffed in it
your old clothes

Nothing to lose but
your pretence in the face of nature
your sentimental twittering drunkenness
your perverse and ideal outbursts
your doors and how they slam shut
your clumsiness

Nothing to lose but
your idea of an idea of a sense of self
your constrained, bartered hours
your newly minted obliquities
your chewed and well-tongued cheeks
your chains, still, after all these attempts,

your chains.

The sea's rising arc

wipes its mouth on our sentimental gaze,
chucks its spume and spleen our way,
till we are forced back to the car.
The children bicker over the head of some toy.

We ignore them. It's cold and getting colder.
On the shore the waves are building to a riot
of pointless fury, mob after justified mob
wanting payback for some ancient grievance.

There are lost souls flying above the sand,
crimped and chapped from desperate scrubbing.
We can even hear them breathing in the car
when the children fall asleep, in the background

to our silence, breath so shallow it's like that
of the man pulled dead from a freezing sea,
just waiting to thaw, only they buried him,
heard him jerk awake, skin his brow on the coffin lid.

We're about to admit something we shouldn't,
but the wind catches it and throws it into the sea.
It's hard to know how you felt so long ago,
but if you can, we do. We start to laugh at ourselves:

the white frenzy the sea knocks itself into
seems almost blue as the windows steam up
and we can't do what we dream of doing
even if the kids are asleep. We just can't.

I'll accept the testimony of the river,

its improbable stories about the future
that lasts forever, the fields now under
the floodwaters. A cloud smothers the moon:
like a security light clicking off.
The river slips its arm around the park

in a drunken gesture of comradeship.
You're always telling me things will work out.
This cold air's slap has stopped me laughing.
The dew starts to bend the grass back, I could
write with my foot an epic poem or wait

to carve it from the dirt on the car boot.
Looking back toward the house I see
the Pelican Crossing run through its
simple sequence like a nervous actor
learning his one line late into the night.

Uncertainties, mysteries, doubts
cluster in what remains of the light,
like the patterns of dust revealed
when a man you were polling leant against his door
and let the brightness of his home interrogate you.

The road is jealous of the river's chat.
At the back of my throat a tiny shadow
mimics these words, fingers twisting, sliding,
cracking though they have no bones.
'All the better to mock you with.'

The family as the first soviet, and other daft ideas,

swim through my lustful yearnings, my jealousy
of the frustrated certainties of the old comrades.
It all saps the imagination: I can't embroider this
into something complicated, but there's an idea I have
that beneath the surface of the town I shop in

there's another that looks the same but feels
different. Where all the stubbornness and bile
hardens into ornately carved bricks describing
the odd shrinking feeling that buried itself deep,
deep within your chest during the adverts.

In the park this morning we sped down the hill
on some old For Sale signs and a huge bin bag,
bounced over compacted snow picking up speed,
yelling and holding on to each other as we hit the fence
at the bottom, erected to protect the fish farm.

Though we battered it with our accelerating feet
and our cries, it tilted but did not fall.
I wanted us to slide on and out over the water,
you with our son, and me with our daughter,
over the frozen river, our gloves rubbed smooth

as we skimmed the ice and headed out
to startle the sheep, anywhere out of here,
with the rest of the country following.
This may be vague, impractical and sentimental,
but it does not feel it.

If I waste time thinking

of how the songs of the clouds
are writing their cheerful selves down river,
full of anger and historic bottom,
striving to make shapes they never quite manage,
how am I going to get down to breakfast?

There's a dog in the middle of the lawn
barking and barking, chipping away
at the nostalgic picture the houses
on the ragged horizon so desperately sketch.
Too small to be threatening, it skirts the garden
translating the sarcastic messages of our cats.

Each morning, gravity has added another line
to your beautiful face. Each has this to say,
in its different and delightful way:
'This woman is knackered but smiles a lot.'
The kids are minor miracles, or earthquakes,
throbbing with inspiration I can only guess at.

'We have run out of granola, it will have to be
toast or nothing,' you shout. The coffee is as bitter
as the news is bland. 'That's how I like to start the day,'
I say, almost joking. If I wasn't aggressive
I don't know what I would be. I'm sorry.
Somewhere in the kitchen a definition of grace is hiding.

We would have a better chance of finding it
if one of our mothers lived round the corner.
By such flat and cardboard details are the
dimensions of our spiritual life confined.
You'd laugh to see me typing the words
spiritual life. I'm laughing now.

Please come in and disturb me.

Song V: What the Doctor Ordered

Trivial conversation
Regular trips to the football
Letting the grass grow over my feet
A flattering shaving mirror
We must be tough on pride
tough on the causes of pride.

A notepad for explanations
A bin to throw them away
Words of unearned self-praise
Broken crockery if required
We must be tough on lies
tough on the causes of lies.

Two pints of Guinness at bedtime
A book with a happy ending
Cheap music that's not quite free
Sweet nothings in someone's ear
We must be tough on bile
tough on the causes of bile.

Not watching the news
Swearing at the news
A picture on the dartboard
If all else fails, psychotropic drugs.
We must be tough on cries
tough on the causes of cries.

Like an illustration in a children's book

the washing drips in the disparate dusk,
an endless hiatus on the paving stones, dot
after hanging dot widening to circles of damp.
The church bell nags stubbornly at the hour,
keen for souls to save. Ours are doomed
to crease like shirts I hang too hurriedly.

We've been searching for something dull,
like an alarm clock, but not that. If we could remember
what it was, we'd at least know where to start.
An hour spent turning the bathroom upside down,
then we're drawn into scrubbing at smudges
of toothpaste eating away at our new varnish.

The smell of nappies has returned from nowhere,
just won't be scratched from beneath our nails.
Creating a new landscape on the patio,
from mud and compost and heaps of daffodils,
in tantrum-filled abstract expressions of joy
the children out-do us at everything.

They skid and run from apple tree to garage
and scream. Not without aggression they push us
against the garage wall so we cannot work.
I have felt forgiveness shrink in me
like an unused organ and been terrified.
I have hidden my anger in folds of wind

but now I am ready to pack away this disillusion.
Look at the last of the sun on the children's legs,
the way it has nothing at all to do with things
more complex than heat, light, smoothness
of skin that has hardly begun to age. Another
enthusiastic misunderstanding I may live to regret.

Sooner or later we must face the pittering crackle

that's the background to living
with this speech in our ears,
going forward firmly not looking to the past
building as individuals a new future, firmly.

That pittering crackle is not our letters
to the papers being burnt unread,
or some decorative celebrations
of one small getting even.

It's not a statement of the obvious
demanding a pat on the back,
or a radio tuned to its inner child,
or tomorrow coming down the phone line.

No. That sound's what's left
of songs forged from static,
and air escaping from ideas
once so tight and firm the bounce

would catch you unawares,
leave you feeling foolish and gauche.
Let's assume false names and
suddenly become intemperate.

Call the lying bastards that
and prove it by what they cause:
lives like broken-backed chairs
people still have to use.

How did we lose sight of it?
We are more imaginative than they are.
This stubborn resistance informs my days.

Walking the gaps between hills

the children are gripped by a sudden calm.
Hand in hand they profess in approximate words
their love for each other, turned by some trick
of this polluted light into giants
striding on our behalf out of this world,
anywhere innocence is not ironic.

The humps of green are melting into autumn,
the odd bare line shyly scratches itself
on our memories of this long hot summer.
In the valley the sky's a day away
and the sea just a persistent rumour.
The horses in the fields aren't at all puzzled.

As the slope steepens we can see the kids'
legs start to bend with the effort, as if
the statues we would make of them were top heavy,
had legs of papier maché and torsos of stone.
We scoop them up and driven impulsive by hope
race them screaming to the top of the hill.

Nature, someone else's Great Lost Cause,
tries to underline the lesson of all this,
but I'm too stupid to see it. I can feel
my life gathering pace like a stone dislodged
by our running, tumbling down the hill,
desperate for a use to put its falling weight to.

Rolled on the floor and still laughing we look down
on the towns below us, the coils and knots of pipes
and chimneys, the clouds of smoke that seamlessly
knit into the sea-fret, terraces like dominoes
waiting to fall in spectacular sequence, the finale
to a festival we are all invited to.

One fitful night after a trying evening

you dream there's this one life and all you have to do
is open the door to find it there on the step,
fresh and fashionable as a milk bottle full of orange juice.
The unanswerable hunger you wake with is deadly,

the day's an idea dismissed as unreasonable
and there's nothing surprising about the news any more.
The bedspread lies in argumentative knots
over clothes performing poor impressions of our charms.

It matters we remember what we were feeling
when careless we threw them to the floor but we can't.
It matters how we touched then on something
we'd forgotten. It seems to matter that the day

begins like this, opens like the bitter flower
in the white jug on our wooden table, beneath
the window that soaks up the sun like a sponge
licks away spilt white wine and the words that spilt it.

The one life you dream of starts with a squall of children,
of moods and merriment. It's an odd shape, for sure,
but as the day gathers pace and runs away from us, again,
and the summer breaks its fall on the garden,

this naive daub of a life has a power of its own and
the square of sky the window shows is all that we expected,
blue as our eyes, and our children's eyes, endless
as the heat that draws and binds this moment together.

Song VI

Glad up to my elbows
Gladder down to my knees
My chest is a fresh-baked loaf of bread
My brow is crammed with tunes
Is that a hyperbole in your pocket
or are you just pleased to see me?

Glad up to my tonsils
Gladder down to my segs
My skin is a suit called Tingle
My smile is a twist of lime
Is that a metaphor in your pocket
or are you just pleased to see me?

Glad up to my earlobes
Gladder down to my calves
My spleen is a stone to sit upon
My heart is a sea-whipped shell
Is that a paradox in your pocket
or are you just pleased to see me?

Glad up to my screaming
Gladder down to my moans
My eyes suck juice from oranges
My hands sculpt great promises
Is that a smirk in your pocket
or are you just pleased to see me?

Bringing Down the Government (Epilogue – 1997)

The wicker chair we'd seen by the skip was gone.
I sat in the space we'd cleared for it and watched
as you topped and tailed the peas, nipping the ends
with the scars you call your fingernails. We cursed
our luck, our place in things, the sods that beat us
to this rare chance to better ourselves. We laughed.

The lifestyle issue, raised again, got laughed
out of the crumbling house, but now it's gone
we want it back – somehow it means a lot to us.
Knowing how much we watch our lives, how watched
they sour like gooseberry wine that's cursed
to turn to vinegar before the summer ends,

when the peas are done we walk to the ends
of our lands, some twenty-five yards of laughed-
and lived-in ground. The children have cursed
the garage with scribble that will soon be gone.
Our daughter waves from the tree, she watched,
she tries to say, while we thought only of us,

the day before yesterday when there was only us.
So this reverie and its quiet talk ends
and we return to the case at hand, watched
by her eager eyes that flashed and laughed
their way through the morning that's now gone.
When we look back, maybe these days will seem cursed

by over-ambition. Still, the only curse
apparent's the one that rips time from us.
The restraint that plagued us suddenly gone
we realise we didn't notice it end.
Did it simply dissolve while we laughed
at it, or did it slip away as we watched

for each other's tensions and oddities, watched
for the signs of silently becoming cursed
to live out ordinary days, the ones we laughed
our way out of when younger? 'It was us
that decided to live like this,' our silence ends
by saying, before the children ensure it's gone.

And if anybody watched the two of us
would we be cursed for the simple ends
we turn our laughed-in lives to? When we're gone?

II

Voice-overs

I   The Boy

We are waiting for the London rain to stop
sucking at our clothes, our dirt-mooned fingernails.
I have stumbled on someone to call Hope,

the shape of a person, bedraggled, pale,
and ripe for dreams of walking into sunsets,
of how warm even a one-bar fire must feel.

Bored beyond tears till her leggings yet
to turn to scrappy fishnets trapped me,
dug up urges I thought had got up and left.

For days, hitching down, she'd seen the city
as a place of anonymous respite.
In this doorway, her fourth night, she found me.

Now we are inventing ways to stay dry.
Preparing to forget to say goodbye.

II   *The Girl*

He has a smile that could catch a fish.
I was dragging my bones up the iron stairs
of the tube when he offered me a wish

if I'd sit by him for fifteen minutes – a dare
almost, something I could never refuse.
Ten minutes later I was beginning to care.

He was turning into something else to lose.
The dirt under his fingernails was ancient,
it was years since he'd a sniff of good news,

but his eyes told me he was innocent.
The way he offered his cider round
and talked of films and what they meant

told me he was looking to be found.
Told me I ought to stick around.

III

She wears a fringed suede jacket that reeks of dope,
from the van, she says, that took her from somewhere
near Leeds to south of the Watford Gap.

The bloke wanted almost nothing in return.
She looks away down toward the river when
she tells me that, like the secret's not even hers.

She turns around and asks me yet again
just why I'm here and not some place better.
I've no answer that's not a lie, so bend

the truth to something funny but bitter,
that she can believe if she wants to.
Her past we have silently agreed to forget.

Her one desire is to go to the zoo.
She tells me she enjoyed *Terminator 2*.

IV

All that's left in the empty catfood dish
he's constantly turning and winking towards
is a thin dime, an inch of rain and some foolish

children's toy from the bag where he hoards
lost things to make Joe Public feel bad
for abandoning his troublesome wards.

They're nothing to the look in his eyes – sad,
and then something out the other side,
a calmness that a too-swift look thinks mad,

in a desperate hurry to make the day decide
what's to happen. I want to help him win.
I want to pick up his bed and make him ride

away, away and never come back again.
I want one day for us to be not quite so thin.

V

Couldn't buy a penny chew in a bankrupt sale
with the interest on her life's small change,
but there's a curve to her voice some men would sell

their blood for, a tilt to her brow that's strange
when she asks a question of a woman in a hat
the shape and colour of strawberry blancmange.

When London's last bowler sticks his brolly out
to poke her, the rush knits my head to his nose
and the pain and his screaming make me feel proud

as we leg it through the queues for the shows.
Les Mis are up in arms for the millionth time.
We are having a ball right now.

Hand in hand we flee the scene of the crime,
draw a short, sweet thin black and bruise-blue line.

VI

The rain tries to make something near to a splash
to wash the heat from panic that won't subside,
that still burns our lungs long after the crash

out of something less fresh to this other side.
'Badlands', he says. Springsteen's 'Nebraska'.
The pictures in his head run 'Bonnie and Clyde'.

The rings round his eyes when I asked the
question about what next seemed to throb.
On the station steps there was a busker

scraping away at a degenerate Bob
Dylan song. He ran his darkening fingers
through his wayward hair and sobbed.

While the lousy voice of the desperate singer
totted up the pittance 'Heaven's Door' would bring her.

VII

And all the passers-by pass by looking pale,
as we empty our pockets and count to ten –
make a pile for silver, one for copper, a pile

for rubbish and one for treasure, and then
blow the whole lot on two coffees and a cake,
before starting to save for tomorrow again.

Her left eye, so blue, squints when she's on the make.
If every word she said was true, I'd weep
and ask the corner to take her back

wherever she came from, to catch her and sweep
those sketchy limbs to a comfortable bed,
to a quieter place on a more stable map.

She smiles at something stupid I've just said.
For some reason she's painted her lips cherry red.

VIII

They have nightmares of how this comes to them
but it never will for their lives are so shrunken
they would rather die. Still, there are some

whose parents will kick it and whose drunken
bereavements will bring them here to shout.
The former chemist, as cheerless as a monk and

as thin as his hair, lost it all, was out
on his ear, is desperate to talk of it,
gets himself a shiner and us all left with nowt

as some scallies have some fun on a day trip.
We go hungry, feed off ourselves all the more,
his jokes, anger, my boxed-in attempts to strip.

He sings a song about a green door
as my shirt and pants fall to the floor.

IX

One day in the not too distant it will
be a moving story that our beautiful kids
will occasionally ask us to tell.

Me, Travis Bickle played by Chaplin,
and her a northern Béatrice Dalle,
soundtrack a souped-up Patsy Cline.

One day we'll look back on this and it will all
seem funny, but till then, we're stuck with pennies
that fall so slowly it's as if they're ill,

that seem to recoil from where we have to live,
a sinking city that will not flood our hearts
no matter how hard it rains, how very little it gives.

One day something better will start.
And then it will try to not fall apart.

X

She wants to be with us more than him
but that punter can pay for shoes for her son.
We walk through the park so the grim

sight can't bother us, and it's almost fun
for a while, but we get to feeling ashamed
we didn't sneak up and batter the runt

and split his filthy money three ways.
It's a sign of health, he says, this caring.
A sign of some sort of growing up, he says.

I don't believe it. He's charming me, but not daring
to go out and act on it. It's a sham.
The look on my face gets him swearing

but I can't help being what I am.
I've had my fill of caring and don't give a damn.

XI

He is somehow content with his lot.
A Cavalier shag with a schoolgirl
who'll do it for twenty and no condom

is the lowlife highlight of his world
this week. We'd like to help this girl but
the leaves in the trees in the park are curled

with rain that might drip down our necks and get
us so excited we pass out. Possible.
But unlikely, hearing the mad dreams she's got.

I've an urge to ditch her, an awful, awful
itch in the middle of my dirty back,
that can't be reached, and won't be told.

But her smile sneaks though a tiny crack;
her smile returns and brings me back.

XII

We are looking from the dry out of the rain
and the day has been kinder than it needed.
The sun sets out like a foreign train

but our troubles and talks have succeeded
in worming out lies and truths I was sneaking
to bury – till a twitch in his cheek pleaded.

In the wind our poor shelter is creaking
like the bones of the buildings above us,
loose at the seams it is leaking,

while we in the damp become lovers.
We are huddled and happy and ready to lie
about where tomorrow might shove us,

the clouds we can't see don't ask us why,
and the rain keeps falling out of the sky.

XIII

They do not want what we have got.
Inches of dead lager, half of a map of
Bristol, a match box with a dead tiger moth,

the keys to a padlock we don't have,
a handkerchief you could cut yourself with,
stubble, stubborn desire that won't shove off,

francs, pesetas, chewits that children give,
holes in everything, breath like a wolf,
the bedtime tale of the Billy Goats Gruff,

some cheese, the dinky car her brother
stole her, two filthy sexy gobs,
a hat to beg with, three quid, the ghost

of a chance, a thin hungry chance, enough:
something that almost rhymes with love.

XIV

*They do not want what we have got
to settle for, which is more than most,
each other. We are tied now, and that is not*

*nothing, that is something we should toast
with a drink a sight livelier than this beer,
at a party only the streets could host.*

*Sam the Sham grins from ear to ear
in his leather jerkin and fisherman's boots,
kisses Mable, for once without fear,*

*blushing and shaking to her roots.
A party without thought for our past,
something we have earned: to be pissed as newts.*

*We would not have got this if we'd asked
and tomorrow we will see that it lasts.*

XV *The Director*

We are waiting for the rain to stop.
He has a smile that could catch a fish.
She wears a fringed suede jacket that reeks of dope.

All that's left in the empty catfood dish
couldn't buy a penny chew in a bankrupt sale.
The rain tries to make something near to a splash

and all the passers-by pass by looking pale.
They have nightmares of how this comes to them,
one day in the not too distant it will.

She wants to be with us more than him.
He is somehow content with his lot.
We are looking from the dry out of the rain.

They do not want what we have got.
They do not want what we have got.

III

I know too much
To be anything any more;
And if in the distant

Future someone
Thinks he has once been me
As I am today,

Let him revise
His insolent ontology
Or teach himself to pray.

Derek Mahon

Annaghmakerrig Kelpie

A kelpie is a water spirit said to lure travellers to their deaths.

Bellies full but wanting inspiration
to clear their heads of spirits marshalling
words or colours into striking line
they come down from The Big House.
The water stays where the lake sets it,
though the rain makes it swell, and the wind
crinkles it to crêpe, silvered by the moon.
I move inside the lapping near their sensitive
feet and slap against stones like tentative
applause, from an uncertain audience.
Sometimes I'll pick the windiest of these blow-ins,
and when the clouds close in and damp tightens
to the first signs of rain, I'll take the shape
of a dog or even, for the more romantic,
a deer, and follow them up and through the gorse,
only ever half-appearing, turning
my shy face to their inquisitive eyes
as they turn and wonder, wander round the mud
they don't dare get on their shoes, and up again
to The Big House where I'll shift into the cat
that bothers them for bacon rind, or a sniff
of camomile, or a peek in the dictionary.
Spooked, by they don't know what, they wait
anxiously, eagerly, to empty the dishwasher.
I slip back into the lake and sing to the moon
of my unique benevolence.

Crossroads

after Robert Desnos

In the grip of the grid of yellow lines
cornered by traffic lights, he turns up
his hand before a fine morning,

judging its weight and tone of voice.
The sky is so clear, a cloud would seem
too cute to swallow, a touch vulgar.

The song at the heart of his life whistles
down the street peering in windows,
asking questions of passing faces.

The town on the horizon, traffic buzzing,
is awash with people already, ringing
with noises like a bell, ringing.

The day is so true to itself it enters
his eyes, heart, cheeks, trousers,
shoes, feet, wallet and new haircut,

so that he just has to laugh out loud,
at the world and his town, and the wind swinging
the leaves about in front of the library.

The smell from the pizzeria makes him laugh,
and the hotdog-sellers frying onions,
and the cars stopped near the theatre.

As he enters the pedestrian zone
he sees the girl, she appears from nowhere,
ankles and knees perfectly balanced.

And she laughs too, and carries on
as she passes him and disappears,
and the birds and traffic sing a new song.

Michael

From the corner of the Rec that gently tips the road
down into the town that would swallow his village whole
he could still at that time see right through it,
the way his mother said she could see daylight
pouring in one of his ears and out the other,
from the Con Club past the library, to where
the fields started to interfere with the roads.

While he slept the books by his bed pushed on,
when he woke he could open his mouth and sing along
to a tune that was saying goodbye to all this,
and stoned once on the Rec he saw the sky thrash
itself into a thousand new colours and shapes
as a fox showed him ways to avoid bad trips
and how to find faith to build upon.

A teacher now, he uses his mother's daylight
quip to put bright kids in their rightful place.

Sally

Not satisfied with the shape of her world
she whittles it down to a choice between
the little black dress and the endless night
spent once on the docks with the veal protest.
At weekends she's so glad of the rest
from work she spends it on a losing fight
with sleep that wipes her mind shockingly clean
of the dreams she has of herself as a girl.

She would ride her bike around the block
until the boys began to whistle at her,
until, pouting like a goddess, she'd brake
to a halt six inches from the big one's gate
and demand to be told what was the matter.
Couldn't they control their tiny cocks?

She wakes up sweating, feeling somehow good.
She wouldn't swap now for then if she could.

Laying a Carpet With My Dad

We squeezed the settee out to the dining room
then rolled up the old carpet and flopped it on the stairs
to lie there till bin day like a subject we'd had to drop.

Feeding the shiny white banister through my hands
I ran up to my room or to the loo along its back.
The foam cracked and fell off, like scabs I picked at.

The Stanley knife was so sharp I was forbidden to touch.
Along the spikes of the Betagrip I ran my fingers
till I had scratched new patterns on the tips, the prints.

We rolled out the fragrant new carpet in strict rhythm,
counting, as if learning to dance, so that it didn't slant,
revealing more of the pattern with each movement.

Dad whipped round the edges trimming the excess and then
we set to pulling and pushing it to that taut perfection
my Mum expected. Nothing of a job, but satisfying.

The knee-kicker was an instrument of torture
you could fall in love with, for the give of the cushion
as you punched it forward, the grip of the pins, silver, not letting go.

Dad and I would sit in the middle of the empty room
and try to ignore the corner where the carpet did not quite reach.
That was where we would put the settee.

Crossing the road, Mum would say,

is not like in your silly cartoons.
Once flattened, real children don't get up.
When she let go of my hand opposite
the bus stop I was Speedy Gonzalez,
small, excitable, Mexican, free.
To the newsagents for a Marathon.

At playtime I shared it with Pete Hayes
as we got excited over *My Dingaling*,
deaf to the bells, or the alarm
the very idea set off in our parents.
Pete sang *Long Haired Lover from Liverpool*
as if he was from Salt Lake City, not
the wrong side of the wrong playing fields,
and a family who swore in front of him.

Standing now at that bus stop starting block
I'm married, visiting home but driven
to escape from endless photos of myself
and the lover I brought back from Liverpool,
and our children – whose hands my mother
will not drop this long Bank Holiday Weekend –
I see that highly-strung mouse re-run, sprint
the marathon over The Bridges to school,
away from his mother – *Andelez, Andelez* –
all the way to his eleven-plus.

(And then, that first Grammar School morning,
newly uniformed and cardboard briefcased,
with a tie the neighbours had never seen before,
my mother waved me off at the bus stop
to the jeers of the sixth-formers at the back.
I saw her cross the road and start to wait
for her bus to work. May she slap my backside
if I'm cutting or changing things for effect –
for I am *not* too big.)

Ceremony

I

A man walks out into a field looking for a tune to hum.
His overcoat is the colour of his wife's pastry when it's
left a few minutes too long. He's thinking about his daughter
and the dissolute life he fears she lives at University.
The horizon is a blackening of hedgerows behind
his late September shadow. In his pocket he plays with stones
he's had since he was thirteen. He reaches the field set aside
to do nothing in and offers up a prayer for his daughter,
starts to bury a small black box of dirt in the fine soil,
breaking the earth with his hands, patting it flat again after.

At his kitchen sink, scrubbing the black earth from beneath his
    nails,
as his wife proudly lifts from the oven a pie without
even a tinge of brown, even around the fluted edges,
he starts to whisper a circular tune that goes on all night.

II

Eighteen, she reverses the car down the long path to the road
without turning her head, plunges backwards into the picture
held in the rear-view mirror, the white gate shining in the dusk.
She swings the car round sending stones skidding into the grass
and then follows her full beam into the dark. A healthy sneer
competes with a smile just beneath the pale surface of her face.
The night and the car combine, an hour she experiences
as a memory even as she moves so swiftly through it.

The town throws its cheap necklace of street lights up to catch
behind its back, places it carefully around her neck
as she accelerates through amber near the iron works.
She is singing along to a record the radio played
a mile back, when she was still alone in the dark, travelling
through her own thoughts, feeling a stranger on these familiar
    roads.

III

She stands at the kitchen door and watches them go, each
    leaving
some presence around the table, mud from his boots, her
    perfume.
She traces the boundaries of her land, the outside edges
of fields whose neatness is almost an obsession, almost
the only reason he heaves himself from their bed most mornings,
while she is up and about setting yeast to bubble and bread
to rise and fill the room with the smell of a contented home.
She looks without affection at the table where she breakfasts
alone, sits down at it and rubs her palms against the grain,
runs a nail down the cracks to remove some drying pastry.

She lowers and turns her head, lays it on her forearms as if
someone was stood behind her rubbing her shoulders with his
    thumbs.
Her hands that had been fists open, her eyes close, she starts to
    dream
while the oven creaks and the rest of the house holds its silence.

Mystic at Breakfast, Annaghmakerrig

'No,' he explains somewhat impatiently,
as if we are being a little slow on the uptake,
'I can literally see there is a nerve trapped,
nipped, between two vertebrae, it's that
that is giving the stomach trouble.'
It's to do, it seems, with looking objectively,
knowing the right questions to ask
the pendulum, and then just looking properly.

We all look towards Angela's stomach.

She has a blue sweater on, ribbed,
clean. If you stare very hard, impolitely
hard, you might just see small breaths
being taken, the T-shirt underneath
through the holes. No, she says,
she doesn't have trouble with her neck.
He finds *this* hard to believe.

If he's right, I'm surprised he doesn't
mention the negative vibrations
the episode sets off in my aura,
and the aura around my muesli,
or comment on the thinness of the veil
between the flat dimension of my face
and the pure spirit of the smirk beneath.

I leave the table holding the mysteries
of my dry life in, like a fit of giggles.

Mistaken Identity

I was mistaken for the sole of a sixteen-hole Doc
worn shiny by use, taken for recycling,
bought in a skip-load by a middle-aged artist
for a messy sculpture about his quicky divorce.
I remember being glued onto the forehead
of an ungrateful showroom dummy.

I was mistaken for a goldfish not moving,
idling near the murky bottom of its bowl.
I was poked and pushed in circles as if that would
set my fins flapping again, make me dance.
The ceiling was huge. I remember feeling dizzy,
having to make myself sick to make the feeling go away.

I was mistaken for a sharpened stick scratched out
of a length of unpainted woodchip near a teenager's bed,
catching beneath the nail of his long index finger,
causing mayhem when he picked his nose on the sly.
There was blood everywhere. I remember being wiped off
and swallowing for ever more the darkness under his mattress.

I was mistaken for tea leaves blocking the kitchen sink,
and for the finger freezing under the cold tap to push them away.
I remember what the garden looked like,
when the drains finally backed up.
The green of the lawn and trees pulsated,
like a close-up in a film about heart surgery,
but in green, not red. I remember not wanting to go.

I was mistaken for the cracked spine on a paperback Chambers
    English Dictionary.
I was mistaken for the plastic sheath on a nine-inch Sabatier
    kitchen knife.
I was mistaken for Bert Hardy's first lens cap.
I was mistaken for a floppy disc stepped on by a dog, forever
    stumm.
I was mistaken for the last grain of salt on Friday night's chip
    paper
and for the cabbage in a misjudged, too-late kebab that turned
    into a fight.